RAILWAYS IN THE NORTH AMERICAN LANDSCAPE

MIKE DANNEMAN

AMBERLEY

First published 2021

Amberley Publishing
The Hill, Stroud
Gloucestershire, GL5 4EP

www.amberley-books.com

Copyright © Mike Danneman, 2021

The right of Mike Danneman to be identified as the Author
of this work has been asserted in accordance with the Copyrights, Designs and
Patents Act 1988.

ISBN 978 1 3981 0392 4 (print)
ISBN 978 1 3981 0393 1 (ebook)

British Library Cataloguing in Publication Data.
A catalogue record for this book is available from the British Library.

Origination by Amberley Publishing.
Printed in the UK.

INTRODUCTION

My father, and many of my older friends that enjoyed railroading before I was born, were exposed to trains in an incredibly different setting than I was. Some of them were old enough to experience the last of the steam locomotives in regular service, along with the roundhouses, coaling and water towers and workforce used to support these incredible machines. Even after the end of steam, they were surrounded by depots and interlocking towers where workers and agents would frequently invite a person into a different world than we know today. Old signals, pole lines, colourful passenger trains and a huge variety of railways and locomotives gave them wonderfully diverse photo opportunities as they grew up into railroad photography.

When I was a young boy, I was happy to ride my bicycle a few miles from home to the nearest railroad yard and photograph whatever locomotive or train showed up. By the time I picked up a camera, many of the things that made railroads interesting were already gone, or abandoned and soon would be. I was still able to photograph some railroads that were slow to change, and there was plenty of variety when I first began taking photos. I soon learned to make use of line side props like towers, signals and depots to make photographs more interesting. As I grew older and further travel expanded my horizons, so too did my desire to make a railroad photograph more impactful. I quickly found the railroad in landscapes most captivating.

Travelling across the United States and Canada seeing a wonderful diversity of topography can be exhilarating. A railroad going through the setting is like the proverbial icing on the cake! The array of topography across the continent is what challenged railroad builders centuries ago, but it is also what gives photography of those railways its allure.

North America is the third largest continent in the world, and has wonderfully diverse physical geography and environment. In the east, the Atlantic coast is home to many large population centers. The Atlantic coastal plain sees beaches, rivers and wetlands extending west to the base of a mountain range. North America's older mountain ranges, such as the Appalachians, rise along the eastern coasts of the United States and Canada, and were a formidable obstacle to early railroad builders forging

westward into a new frontier. These mountains have been mined for rich deposits of coal and other minerals for hundreds of years, and the coming of the railroads brought easier transportation of goods.

To the north, the Canadian Shield is a low, rocky plateau that extends over a huge area of Canada, along with northern portions of the states of Michigan, Wisconsin and Minnesota. The Shield is one of the world's richest areas of mineral ores, and many rail lines were built in the region to reach numerous mining towns.

In the middle of the continent is the Great Plains, where deep, rich soil blankets these flat areas of Canada and the United States. Known as the 'Breadbasket of North America', grain grown in the region also feeds a large part of the world, with railroads moving the important staple to ports on the Great Lakes and west coast. The Great Plains are also home to rich deposits of oil, natural gas and coal. Over the years, Wyoming's Powder River Basin has shipped out astounding amounts of coal in unit trains, which are freight trains carrying a single type of commodity.

Heading westward over the prairies brings one abruptly to the continent's young mountains rising in the west. The most familiar of these ranges is the Rocky Mountains, which extend from British Columbia through the western states south to northern New Mexico, forming North America's largest mountain chain. Other smaller parallel ranges cover much of the western part of the continent, while some of the earth's youngest mountains are the Cascade Range of Washington, Oregon and California. All of these mountains challenge the railroads that were audacious enough to forge steel paths through tunnels, passes and canyons of the west.

These extraordinary mountain ranges have 'rain shadows' that have created astonishing desert regions in North America. Many times overlooked as 'wasteland', these desert areas are very unique and have a beauty of their very own. Railways crossing the desert country in Utah, or flying across the Mojave Desert in California, look like they could be crossing the landscape of the moon.

Even though the railway scene today is so different – with much bigger railroads and less variety, more sterile surroundings and stringent trespassing rules – railroad landscapes are still out there. However, even those can change with more private property and foliage growth. I still think it is these vastly varied landscapes across the continent that makes capturing railways in their environments in photographs so interesting to me. Although I have been photographing trains for quite a while, I still really enjoy getting out and capturing a new image of a railroad in an amazing landscape. There are still many new places I'd like to see and photograph.

All of the photos in this book were made by myself from 1988 to 2018 using both film and digital formats. In early film days, I used Kodachrome 64 and 200, and Fujichrome 100F and 400F films using Pentax cameras, while in the digital era I rely on Canon equipment. But truth be told, I don't believe that film and camera choices are really as important as being out there with friends and family, enjoying the time outdoors, and getting some good photographs with a little practice and patience.

Just like many of the railway builders centuries ago that constructed their railroads westward, I too arranged the photos in this book to go roughly from east to west. As you turn these pages I wish you a pleasant trip across the continent as you look at railways in the North American landscape.

Springtime in the Berkshires

Conrail's FRSE-2 freight passes milepost 129 on the old B&A line west of Chester, Massachusetts. May 1993.

Northeast Corridor electrics

An AEM7 electric locomotive powers an Amtrak passenger train through Elizabeth, New Jersey. May 1993.

Along the Hudson

A Conrail stack train crosses Popolopen Creek Bridge along the Hudson River at Fort Montgomery, New York. April 1991.

Cruising toward Breakneck Ridge

An Amtrak Rohr Turboliner sprints along the Hudson River past Pollepel Island's Bannerman Castle approaching Breakneck Ridge, New York. April 1991.

View from Maryland Heights

Fog has finally lifted as Amtrak's *Capitol Limited* heads east across the Potomac River departing Harpers Ferry, West Virginia. October 1990.

Homeward bound

A Maryland Area Rail Commuter train crosses the Potomac River into Harpers Ferry, West Virginia, April 1996.

Autumn in the Allegheny Mountains

Amtrak train 40, the *Broadway Limited*, glides downgrade through Horseshoe
Curve west of Altoona, Pennsylvania. October 1988.

Conrail pushers

A pair of Conrail EMD SD40 locomotives push hard on a westbound freight entering Horseshoe Curve near Altoona, Pennsylvania. October 1988.

Rain and colour

A CSX freight train powered by a trio of former Chessie System EMD GP40s curves through Mance, Pennsylvania. October 1988.

San Sebastian crossing

Florida East Coast train 226-10, with brand-new GE ES44C4s, crosses the
San Sebastian River at St. Augustine, Florida. January 2015.

Pocahontas District coal train

A man and his dog rest in the shade of the UMWA building in Keystone, West Virginia, as a Norfolk Southern coal train rumbles by. May 2014.

Virginia farm country

Norfolk Southern train 38Q is eastbound through Crockett just east of Rural Retreat, Virginia. May 2014.

Naturally carved by Stock Creek

An eastbound CSX coal train eases out of the 100-foot-high Natural Tunnel at Glenita, Virginia. May 2014.

Clinchfield territory

Two EMD SD50 locomotives power a southbound CSX freight over Copper Creek Viaduct at Speers Ferry, Virginia. October 1990.

Running Southern style

Norfolk Southern train 180 led by a trio of high-nose EMDs is at Tateville, Kentucky, on the former Southern Railway 'Rathole' line. August 1992.

Cumberland River crossing

A northbound Norfolk Southern grain train, No. 114, crosses the big bridge at Burnside, Kentucky. June 1994.

From a precarious perch

High above the rugged shores of Lake Superior, Canadian Pacific train 935 curves through Mink Tunnel near Coldwell, Ontario. September 1993.

On a frosty morning

A westbound Conrail double stack intermodal train heads for Chicago west of New Carlisle, Indiana. February 1990.

One of the busiest interlockings in the world

A Chicago Transit Authority commuter train negotiates a curve past Tower 18 on the elevated at Lake and Wells Street in Chicago, Illinois. November 2018.

Departing Chicago Union Station

Metra No. 199, a unique EMD F40PHM-2, pulls a commuter train out of Chicago, Illinois. November 2018.

Main Line of Mid-America

Illinois Central southbound freight CHG passes a picturesque
barn between Ashkum and Danforth, Illinois. June 1990.

WC stands for Wisconsin Central

Led by a pair of EMD SD45s, a Wisconsin Central ore load approaches
Theresa, Wisconsin. July 1995.

Night moves

Loading and unloading containers on and off trains is a round-the-clock job at Union Pacific's intermodal terminal at Joliet, Illinois. November 2010.

Bridge over Turtle Creek

Chicago & North Western's Janesville to Chicago freight crosses the graceful arched bridge at Tiffany, Wisconsin. August 1995.

Fields of corn

A Santa Fe intermodal train sprints eastbound out of Ancona, Illinois. June 1993.

Tying up traffic on 2nd Street

A southbound Soo Line freight rumbles through the Mississippi River town of Bellevue, Iowa. February 1992.

Along Devils Lake

A circus train heads for Milwaukee on the Chicago &
North Western at Devils Lake, Wisconsin. July 1993.

Autumn in Minnesota

An A-B-B-A set of EMD F9s of LTV Mining Company curves through Cramer with an empty taconite ore train. September 1994.

Lake Superior ore dock

EMD F9 No. 4210 leads a LTV Mining taconite train as it slowly unloads over the dock at Taconite Harbor, Minnesota. September 1991.

Flying over Media Trestle

A Santa Fe intermodal train speeds eastbound at Media, Illinois. May 1986.

Taking a break from fishing

A westbound Burlington Northern autorack train rumbles over the Wisconsin River Bridge east of Prairie du Chien, Wisconsin. July 1995.

Dwarfed by the bean plant

Iowa Traction Railroad electric steeple cab
No. 54 switches the AGP bean plant in
Mason City, Iowa. April 2008.

Amtrak from Dayton's Bluff

The eastbound *Empire Builder* has just departed
St. Paul, Minnesota. June 2016.

Springtime in Iowa

Passing dandelions, an Iowa Northern freight heads
south through Rockford, Iowa. May 2014.

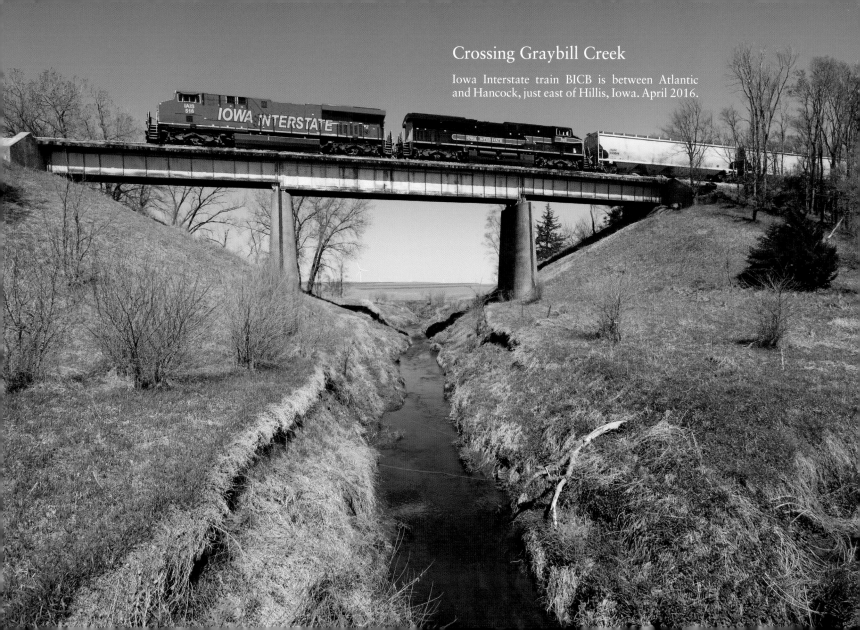

Crossing Graybill Creek

Iowa Interstate train BICB is between Atlantic and Hancock, just east of Hillis, Iowa. April 2016.

Down Main Street

All is quiet in Union, Nebraska, until a southbound Union Pacific passenger train blows through town. September 1995.

Aransas River Bridge

A northbound Kansas City Southern freight crosses the Aransas
River north of Sinton, Texas. March 2013.

Sheyenne River autumn

Burlington Northern EMD SD60M Nos 9205 and 9241 power a coal train over the large bridge at Valley City, North Dakota. October 1996.

Curving over the 'Mighty Mo'

A Burlington Northern coal train crosses the Missouri River between Mandan and Bismarck, North Dakota. June 1994.

Charlie's Lake reflection

Dakota, Missouri Valley & Western's 'wayfreight' reflects in a tranquil
lake north of Garrison, North Dakota. August 2018.

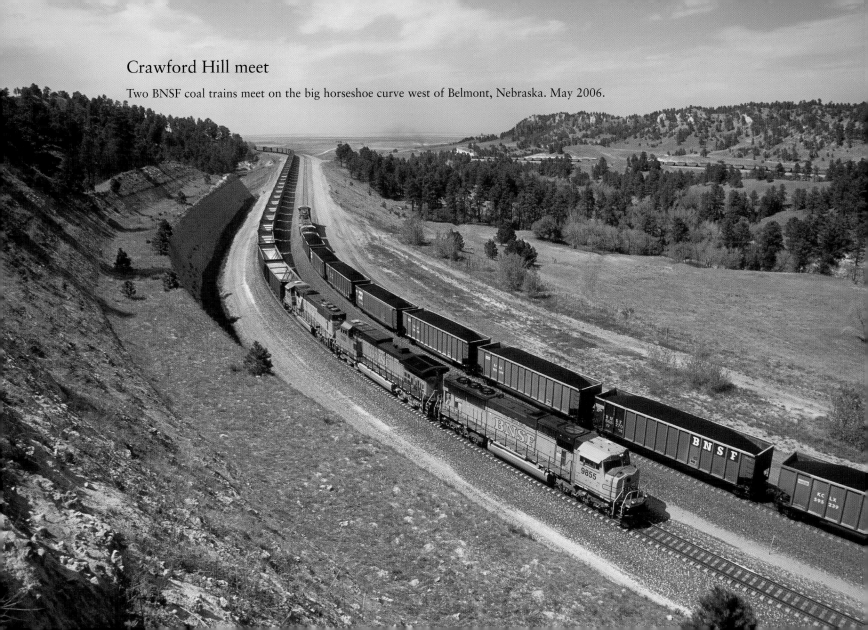

Crawford Hill meet

Two BNSF coal trains meet on the big horseshoe curve west of Belmont, Nebraska. May 2006.

Climbing the hill

Five EMD locomotives power an eastbound Burlington Northern
Santa Fe freight up Crawford Hill, Nebraska. June 2002.

Scenic Wendover Canyon

An eastbound Burlington Northern Santa Fe coal train rumbles along the North Platte River near Wendover, Wyoming. July 1996.

Matching MACs

A trio of EMD SD70MACs power a westbound BNSF coal train over a small trestle in the confines of Wendover Canyon near Cassa, Wyoming. July 1999.

Morning rainstorm

Skirting a quick-moving storm, an eastbound BNSF coal train passes through the North Dakota Badlands at Sully Springs. June 2015.

Snaking through the Badlands

Burlington Northern EMD locomotives power an eastbound coal train at Sully Springs, North Dakota. August 1991.

Ten degrees of curvature

Leaving the Great Plains behind, a Union Pacific coal empty climbs around Big 10 Curve and through Clay, Colorado. October 2011.

Heading for the slopes

Coal Creek Canyon is covered in a nice coat of snow as the Rio Grande Ski Train approaches Tunnel 1 east of Plainview, Colorado. March 2001.

Tunneling through the Flatirons

An eastbound coal train, powered by Southern Pacific GE AC4400CWs, exits Tunnel 4 and threads Tunnel 3 at Plainview, Colorado. March 1997.

Ascending Zephyr

Fresh colours of springtime have reached the front range as Amtrak's *California Zephyr* climbs the two per cent grade west of Plainview, Colorado. June 2013.

After a winter storm

Clouds still cling to the lower mountaintops as four Southern Pacific GE AC4400CWs haul an empty coal train through Crescent, Colorado. March 1998.

Curving through Tunnel 29

Union Pacific's executive passenger train roars through Tunnel 29 and heads for Pinecliffe, Colorado. June 1998.

Windswept Wyoming

Looking through snow fences lining the tracks to protect the railroad from wind-driven snow, a Union Pacific freight ascends Sherman Hill, Wyoming. September 2003.

The rocks of Dale

Crossing Sherman Hill, a westbound Union Pacific unit potash train is approaching Dale Junction, Wyoming. September 2008.

Hermosa Tunnels

A westbound Union Pacific intermodal train curves out from one of the twin bores of Hermosa Tunnels at Hermosa, Wyoming, September 2003.

End of a stormy day

In Wyoming's Powder River Basin, a BNSF coal train heads south out
of Bill at the close of a rainy day. May 2007.

Wide open spaces

Under a sky erupting with thunderstorms, a southbound BNSF train is about to crest Logan Hill, Wyoming. July 2016.

Curving through Abo Canyon

Two classes of Santa Fe EMD GP60s pull a westbound freight through Abo Canyon at Sais, New Mexico. September 1992.

Hustling westbound

A Santa Fe intermodal train dashes over Bridge 874.2 at the west end of Abo Canyon at Sais, New Mexico. June 1995.

Warbonnets and cactus

Four Santa Fe GE B40-8Ws speed an eastbound intermodal train out of Sais, New Mexico. May 1991.

Colorado's Tennessee Pass

Beneath lofty 14,000-foot peaks, a Rio Grande freight climbs the east slope of Tennessee Pass at Keeldar, Colorado. July 1990.

Red Gorge passage

A crevice that was created by the Colorado River offers passage to BNSF's Denver to Provo freight west of Radium, Colorado. November 2012.

In colourful Red Canyon

Westbound on the Dotsero Cutoff, a Union Pacific passenger special is between Dell and Range, Colorado, September 2000.

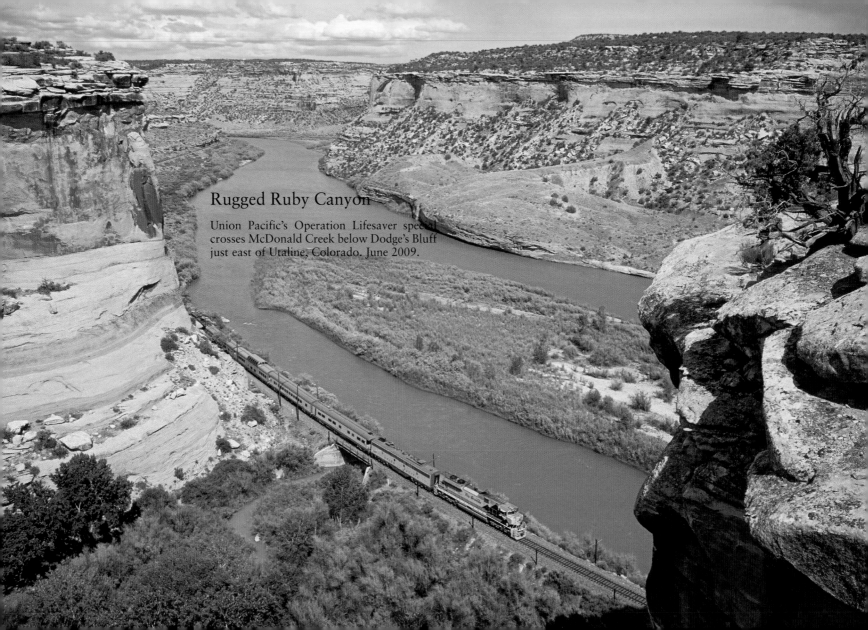

Rugged Ruby Canyon

Union Pacific's Operation Lifesaver special crosses McDonald Creek below Dodge's Bluff just east of Utaline, Colorado. June 2009.

Black Tunnel

Northbound BNSF freight HDENLAU passes through 370-foot Black Tunnel south of Dornick in Wyoming's picturesque Wind River Canyon. June 2018.

Vista at Sheep Canyon

BNSF's Cowley turn snakes through remote and spectacular
Sheep Canyon near Greybull, Wyoming. June 2016.

Remarkable environs

Tracing the Bighorn River, BNSF's Cowley turn exits wonderfully stark Sheep Canyon north of Greybull, Wyoming. June 2017.

Himes Canyon panorama

A southbound BNSF manifest freight follows the Bighorn River between Kane and Himes, Wyoming. June 2018.

Tight curve

Bending around a sharp curve leading into Himes Canyon is a northbound BNSF freight leaving Himes, Wyoming. June 2017.

High country desert electrics

Deseret Power Railway's unit coal train passes milepost 31 near Bonanza, Utah. October 2015.

Track squiggles

Union Pacific's Potash local approaches
Emkay, Utah, through some curvy track.
March 2012.

Red rock country

Union Pacific's Potash local is about to enter scenic Bootlegger Canyon near Moab, Utah. February 2006.

Lunar-like landscape

Approaching Floy, Utah, is Amtrak's *California Zephyr* in a view from the bordering Book Cliffs. August 1996.

Along the old Lincoln Highway

A Union Pacific stack train descends Peru Hill as seen from inside an abandoned gas station at Jamestown, west of Green River, Wyoming. January 2013.

Arriving at Helper

After crossing the grades of Soldier Summit, Union Pacific's LJP44 local approaches Helper yard. December 2004.

Rio and the Wasatch

A trio of Rio Grande locomotives power a local over Soldier Summit through Rio, Utah, under an eye-popping Wasatch Range. June 2004.

Utah rocks

With the last rays of sun illuminating the scene, a westbound
Utah Railway coal train curves into Rio, Utah. April 2005.

Zipping by some saguaros

Passing some saguaro cactus on the Sunset Route at Wymola, Arizona, is a westbound Southern Pacific intermodal train. April 1990.

Spring in copper country

Copper Basin Railway's ore shuttle train OT-1 exits short Tunnel 2 just east of Ray Junction, Arizona. March 2010.

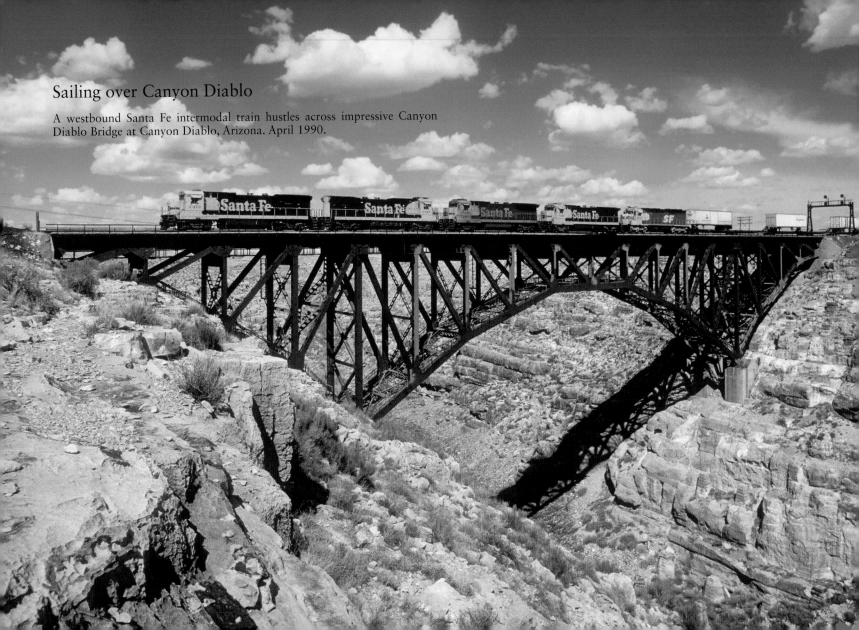

Sailing over Canyon Diablo

A westbound Santa Fe intermodal train hustles across impressive Canyon Diablo Bridge at Canyon Diablo, Arizona. April 1990.

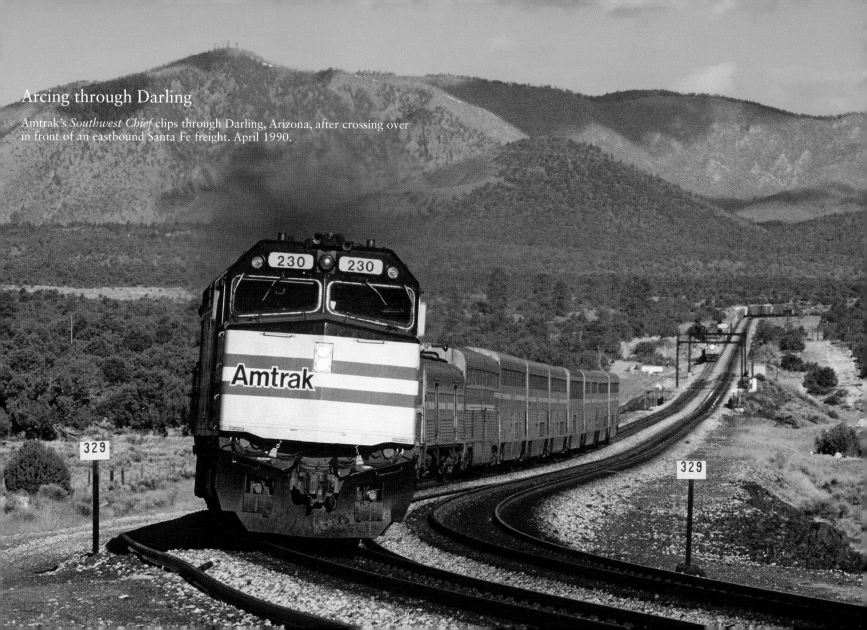

Arcing through Darling

Amtrak's *Southwest Chief* clips through Darling, Arizona, after crossing over in front of an eastbound Santa Fe freight. April 1990.

Steam, sun, snow and shadows

With tiny footprints seen in the glistening snow in a winter field, Union Pacific No. 618 storms by with a freight train at Heber, Utah. February 2006.

Winter in the Heber Valley

Union Pacific 2-8-0 No. 618 hauls a freight toward Edwards Lane where a 1949 Chevy pickup waits for its passing. February 2007.

Meet in Echo Canyon

An eastbound Union Pacific stack train meets a westbound powered by brand-new GE ES44AC No. 7374, east of Echo, Utah. March 2009.

Great Salt Lake crossing

An eastbound Union Pacific freight begins the long trek across Great Salt Lake at Lakeside, Utah. March 2012.

Sun and shadows over Lombard

Heading west along the Missouri River, a BNSF coal train trundles through Lombard Canyon, Montana. June 2018.

Lombard Canyon

With storms surrounding Lombard, Montana, a westbound BNSF coal train snakes along the Missouri River. June 2014.

By the old stock pens

Montana Rail Link's Missoula to Laurel manifest freight rumbles through
Toston, Montana. July 2018.

Working past summer lupines

A BNSF freight led by GE C44-9W No. 5076 climbs Winston Hill passing
milepost 215 east of Winston, Montana. July 2018.

Bearmouth country

Montana Rail Link EMD F45 No. 391 leads the ML freight in Bearmouth Canyon, Montana. September 2003.

Vernal freshness in Glacier

Under the snow-capped peaks of Glacier National Park, a BNSF stack train heads east at Grizzly, Montana. June 2002.

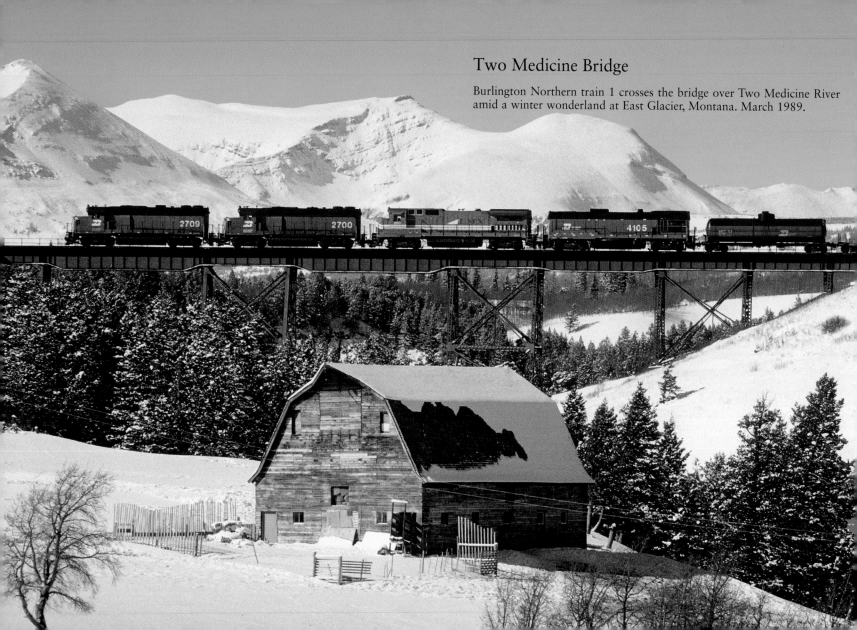

Two Medicine Bridge

Burlington Northern train 1 crosses the bridge over Two Medicine River amid a winter wonderland at East Glacier, Montana. March 1989.

Empire Builder

Climbing over Marias Pass, Amtrak train 8 passes milepost 1148 east of Summit, Montana. June 2002.

Autumn in Glacier National Park

A westbound BNSF stack train crosses Goat Lick Trestle just east of Essex, Montana. October 2018.

Arnold Loop

Near Clifside, a westbound BNSF freight train climbs through Arnold Loop. March 2012.

Framed by high desert flora

Nevada Northern 4-6-0 No. 40 pulls four boxcars and NN caboose No. 5 westbound at Adverse, Nevada. February 2007.

Clear flowing Flathead

Montana Rail Link's gas local heads east along the Flathead
River west of Perma, Montana. September 2012.

Clark Fork reflection

BNSF EMD SD70ACe No. 8595 leads a westbound coal train over the Clark Fork between Thompson Falls and Belknap, Montana. October 2014.

On a crisp winter day

An eastbound BNSF manifest freight crosses the inlet for Trout Creek where it enters the Clark Fork at Trout Creek, Montana. February 2017.

Passing Frog Pond

A father has taken his two small children out in a boat to do some fishing near Trout Creek, Montana, as an eastbound BNSF vehicle train cruises past. May 2013.

Fall in Montana

An eastbound BNSF coal empty passes by Frog Pond at Trout Creek. October 2017.

Over Lake Pend Oreille

On a beautiful summer day, a westbound BNSF intermodal train crosses the bridge over Lake Pend Oreille at Sandpoint, Idaho. June 2006.

Stack in Palisade Canyon

Following the Humboldt River, an eastbound Union Pacific stack train heads toward Palisade, Nevada. March 2012.

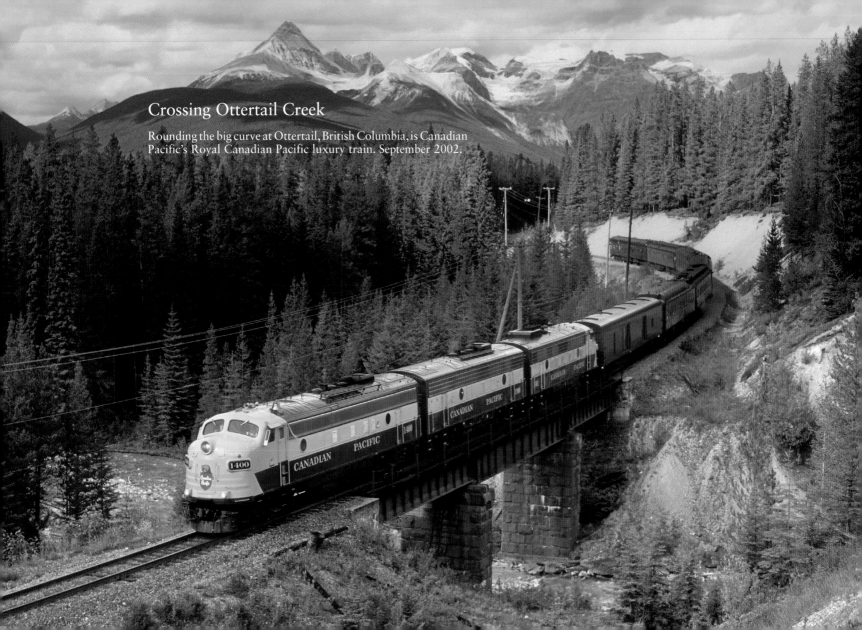

Crossing Ottertail Creek

Rounding the big curve at Ottertail, British Columbia, is Canadian Pacific's Royal Canadian Pacific luxury train. September 2002.

Grain over the Snake

Canadian Pacific GE AC4400CW No. 9620 leads a Union Pacific grain train across UP's massive bridge over the Snake River at Joso, Washington. September 2015.

Hauling Trona

Near Death Valley and passing the Pinnacle National Natural Landmark called the 'Trona Pinnacles', a Trona Railway freight heads toward Searles, California. March 2004.

Marching through the desert

In the Mojave Desert, a Santa Fe freight train passes a Joshua tree west of Jimgrey, California. March 1996.

The Loop

A long Union Pacific freight powered by two EMD SD90MAC-H 6,000 hp locomotives ascend Tehachapi Loop at Walong, California. March 2001.

Meandering through Bealville

A westbound BNSF vehicle train at Bealville, California, has just met another BNSF train that can be seen climbing the grade in the background. February 2016.

Bealville meet

A westbound BNSF freight meets an eastbound (southbound) Union Pacific freight working up the grade into West Bealville, California. March 2016.

Calendar says winter – flowers say spring

Tehachapi Pass is covered with flowers as a BNSF intermodal train climbs into Bealville, California. February 2016.

Above Crater Lake

An eastbound BNSF stack train rounds the basalt cliffs above Crater Lake between Trinidad and Quincy, Washington. September 2016.

Spanning the Columbia

An eastbound BNSF stack train crosses Rock Island Bridge over the
Columbia River between Malaga and Rock Island, Washington. May 2010.

At Windy Point

Traveling through beautiful Jasper National Park, Canadian National train 347 is westbound out of Devona, Alberta. July 2014.

Canadian leaving Swan Landing

VIA Rail train 2, the *Canadian*, rolls eastbound through 'Robertson's Curve' at Swan Landing, Alberta. July 2014.

Black Canyon

A westbound Canadian National intermodal train slinks through the rugged depths of Black Canyon west of Ashcroft, British Columbia. September 2015.

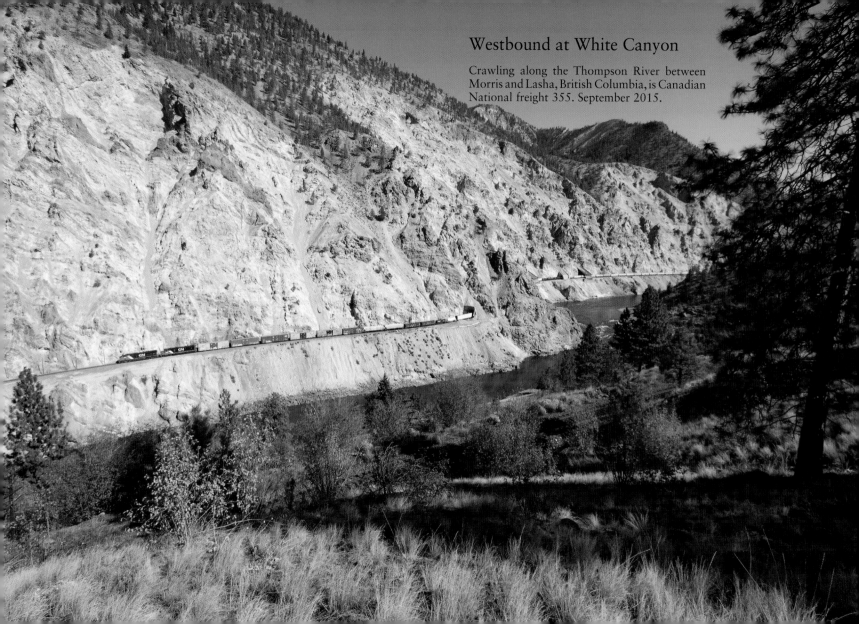

Westbound at White Canyon

Crawling along the Thompson River between Morris and Lasha, British Columbia, is Canadian National freight 355. September 2015.

Keddie Wye

Powered by a trio of GE C40-8 locomotives, a westbound Union Pacific freight curves into Keddie in California's Feather River Canyon. February 1989.

Inside Gateway

A BNSF freight on the 'Inside Gateway' route crosses spectacular Clear Creek Trestle near Keddie, California. March 2000.

Grazing in the Crooked River Valley

Passing a herd of Black Angus cattle, an eastbound City of Prineville Railway train approaches Prineville, Oregon, September 2016.

Crooked River Bridge

A one-car BNSF local heading to Madras crosses the spectacular bridge
located near Terrabonne, Oregon. September 2016.

Leaving Lyle

In the beautiful Columbia River Gorge, a westbound BNSF coal train departs Lyle, Washington. September 2016.

Cape Horn

An eastbound BNSF train exits Cape Horn Tunnel near Washougal, Washington, in the Columbia River Gorge. May 2008.

South Santiam River Bridge

An Albany & Eastern log train crosses the South Santiam River at
Lebanon, Oregon. September 2016.